PICTURE LIBRARY

SKYDIVING

PICTURE LIBRARY
SKYDIVING

Norman Barrett

Photographs by Simon Ward

Franklin Watts

London   New York   Sydney   Toronto

© 1987 Franklin Watts

First published in Great Britain
    1987 by
Franklin Watts
12a Golden Square
London W1R 4BA

First published in the USA by
Franklin Watts Inc
387 Park Avenue South
New York
N.Y. 10016

First published in Australia by
Franklin Watts
14 Mars Road
Lane Cove
2066 NSW

UK ISBN: 0 86313 512 9
US ISBN: 0–531–10352–8
Library of Congress Catalog Card
Number 86–51225

Printed in Italy

Designed by
Barrett & Willard

Photographs by
Simon Ward (with acknowledgment to
    Olympus Cameras and Fuji Film)
Historical pictures:
N.S. Barrett Collection
Science Museum Library
Molly Sedgwick

Illustration by
Rhoda & Robert Burns

Technical Consultants
Tony Butler, Joint National Coach and Safety Officer,
    British Parachute Association
Molly Sedgwick (historical)

Contents

Introduction

Skydiving is the popular name for sport parachuting. Parachutists jump out of airplanes and perform all kinds of maneuvers in the air before they open their parachutes.

In accuracy jumping, they aim to touch down on a small target. In relative work, a team of parachutists link up in special formations in the air as they are falling. In canopy relative work, they link up with parachutes open.

△ A group of parachutists dive out of a plane to begin their descent. This diving from the sky gave skydiving its name.

6

△ In canopy relative work, parachutists build formations with their canopies open. These are modern square, or ram-air, canopies.

▷ An "Aeroconical" student canopy. Beginners use this type of canopy, which is more like the traditional round parachute, because it is easier to operate.

The parachute jump

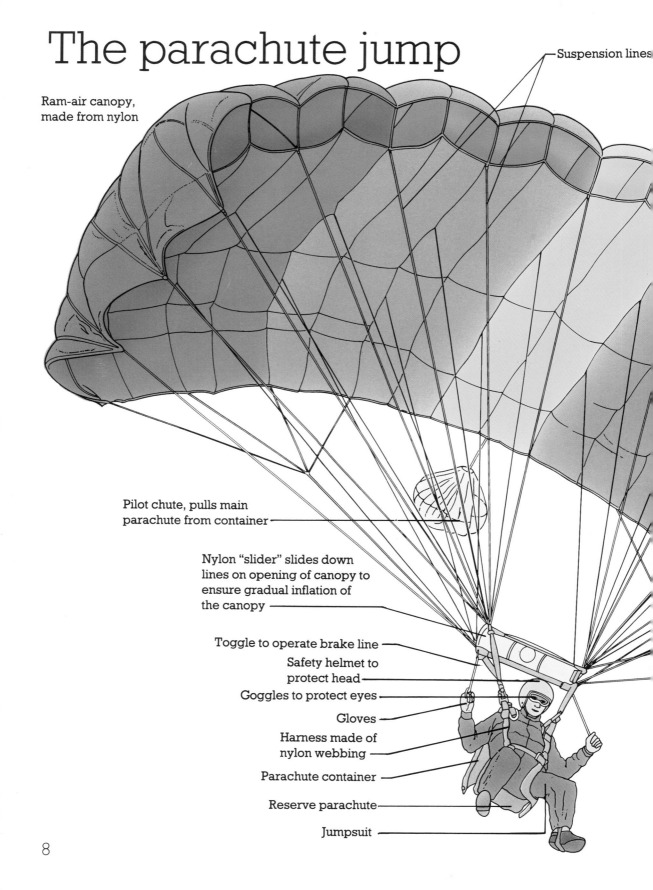

Ram-air canopy, made from nylon

Suspension lines

Pilot chute, pulls main parachute from container

Nylon "slider" slides down lines on opening of canopy to ensure gradual inflation of the canopy

Toggle to operate brake line

Safety helmet to protect head

Goggles to protect eyes

Gloves

Harness made of nylon webbing

Parachute container

Reserve parachute

Jumpsuit

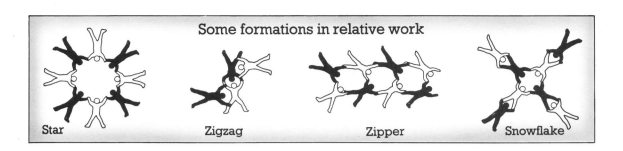

Some formations in relative work

Star   Zigzag   Zipper   Snowflake

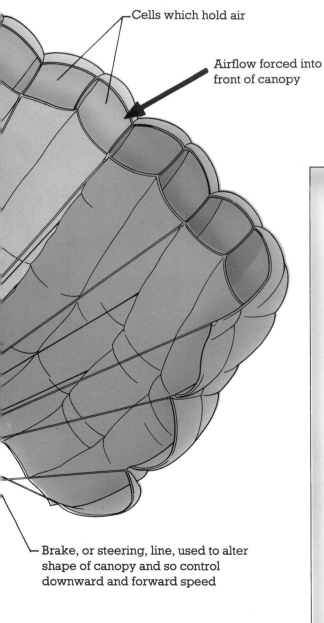

Cells which hold air

Airflow forced into front of canopy

Brake, or steering, line, used to alter shape of canopy and so control downward and forward speed

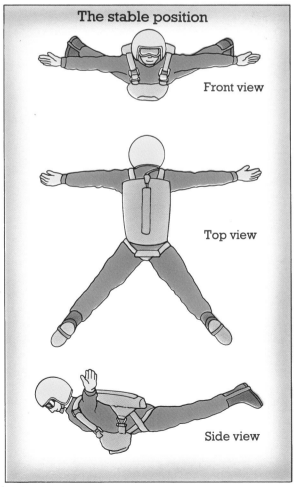

The stable position

Front view

Top view

Side view

Freefall

The part of the jump before the parachute is opened, or deployed, is called freefall.

As any object drops toward earth, it falls faster and faster until it reaches a limit called the terminal velocity. For the average person, this is about 120 mph (195 km/h), reached after about 10 seconds.

At such speeds, skydivers can vary the speed of falling by adopting different body positions.

△ A side and front view of the basic freefalling pose, called the full stable spread position. The back is well arched, the arms and legs are extended, and the head is back. In this position, the skydiver falls facing the earth.

The instrument that can be seen under the right-hand skydiver is an altimeter, which indicates height above the ground.

Skydivers need to be in good shape because freefalling puts somewhat of a strain on the muscles. Slight movements of the body enable the skydiver to perform aerial maneuvers.

▽ The frog position is a relaxed version of the stable position.

Learning to jump

Many parachutists take up the sport just for enjoyment. Parachuting calls for special skills, which come only after practice.

Beginners learn to jump by practicing certain moves and routines on the ground. When they make their first jump, they must be familiar with the parachute equipment and with the basic principles of falling and landing safely.

▽ Ground training is important before students make their first real jump. A beginner, suspended by a harness, practices emergency procedure (left). She is taking out the reserve parachute, which many learners wear at the front. The same student (right) practices the stable position on leaving the mock-up aircraft.

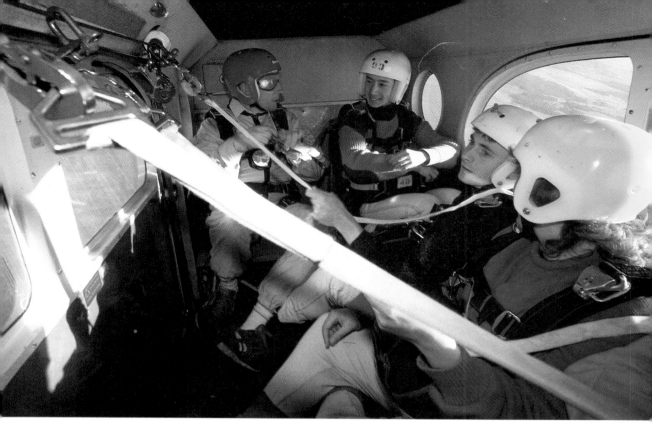

△ Students (yellow helmets) on the way up with their instructor to make what is called a static-line jump. The strong nylon line is attached to the strongpoint of the aircraft (left) by a snap-hook. When the student jumps out, the line, which is attached to the parachute bag, automatically pulls the parachute out.

▷ A student making a static-line jump. The parachute opens automatically.

The static-line method is the usual way for students to make their first jumps. But new methods have been devised so that the student does not have to jump alone.

With a specially designed canopy and double harness, two people can now use the same parachute. This is called tandem jumping.

In a system called accelerated freefall, the learner is accompanied by two instructors during freefall from 10,000 ft (3,000 m) or more.

▽ It is easier to learn the basics of freefall with two instructors holding on to the harness. They can correct faults in body position and even pull the ripcord, if necessary. In this way, a beginner can enjoy the pleasures of freefall during the first jump.

△ Tandem jumping includes a period of freefall.

▷ The instructor deploys the canopy.

▽ With dual-control toggles, the instructor can teach the student how to fly a modern ram-air canopy.

Competition jumping

There are two main types of competition for individual skydivers. These are style and accuracy.

Style is a freefall event where competitors are judged on how they perform set routines. These include turns and back-loops.

In accuracy, the object is to land on, or as close as possible to, a small target on the ground. There are also team competitions for relative work, and canopy relative work.

▷ **An accuracy competitor stretches out a foot toward the target. The target area is a gravel pit with a small disk at the center measuring only 2 in (5 cm) across. Penalty points are given up to a maximum of 500 for a landing 16.4 ft (5 m) or more from the disk.**

▽ **A competitor in a style event performing a back-loop. The judges look for fast, precise maneuvers.**

Relative work

Relative work involves two or more freefallers flying relative to each other. They link up to make all kinds of formations.

The secret of relative work is the ability to speed up and slow down the fall and to track. The tracking position allows a freefaller to cover distance horizontally.

There are competitions in relative work for teams of various sizes.

△ Skydivers making their exit from a DC3. The number taking part in relative work is limited by the size of the aircraft.

The basic skills required for safe relative work can be learned in about 10 jumps. Full control of freefall is necessary to avoid mid-air collisions. Difficult formations may be rehearsed on the ground in what are called "dirt dives."

▷ Two freefallers, combining to display a banner, seem to be attached to their plane.

▽ Setting off canisters of smoke during a group formation adds color to the display.

▷ Building up into a large star formation. The inner group has six members, linking arms in a simple formation. A second ring is built around them, each member docking, or linking, with a leg of one of the inner group and an arm of one of his own group. There are 12 in the second ring. Another ring of 12 is starting to form on the outside, with each member linking to two legs.

A photographer, on the left, captures the display with a helmet-mounted camera. As he needs both arms to control his freefall, he uses a cable release, possibly operated by mouth, for the shutter, and the film winds on automatically.

20

◁ Building up to a really big formation.

▷ The British Army Sport Parachute team (above) complete a "donut flake." Relative work at night (below right) is captured by the photographer's flash. Teamwork and timing must be exact, because there is very little light.

▽ A side view above the clouds shows clearly how members "fly" in to join the formation. Once docked, each member must continue to work to keep the group steady.

Canopy relative work

Linking up in formations with canopies open is called canopy relative work, or CRW. It is sometimes called stacking, because the basic formations involve stacking canopies one above the other.

The normal ram-air canopies are used for CRW, but with modifications for safety and control when in contact with others.

▷ A stack of ram-air canopies makes a colorful picture in the sky. Members of a stack link up one above the other, with their feet hooked under straps connected to the harness below.

▽ Viewing a large vertical stack from above.

CRW is often performed after relative work. But it is not safe to continue under 1,000 ft (300 m), because this does not allow enough time to clear any entanglements.

CRW usually takes place at lower heights than freefall, and the movement is much slower, so it is a colorful spectacle from the ground.

There are also competitive events for CRW teams, including stacking and changing formations.

◁ This diamond canopy formation is much more difficult than it is made to look by experts. It involves linking with the canopies.

▽ In a "downplane," two jumpers fly their canopies away from each other while keeping a body grip. This results in a rapid descent.

The story of skydiving

The first parachutes

The idea of the parachute was known in ancient China thousands of years ago. But it was not until the 1700s in France that the first parachutes were made and eventually used.

An early pioneer of ballooning, Jean-Pierre Blanchard, fixed a huge parachute over the car of a balloon in 1784. There is no record that this was ever used, but it is known that he sent dogs down on parachutes.

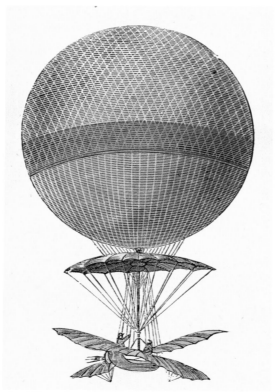

△ Blanchard's balloon, with a parachute fixed over the car.

The first drop

In 1797, another Frenchman, André-Jacques Garnerin, was the first person to make a parachute drop from an aircraft – a gas-filled balloon. He stood in a basket hanging from an open parachute made of silk with a supporting pole. He dropped from about 3,300 ft (1,000 m) over Paris and came down safely.

△ Garnerin makes the first parachute drop in England, in 1802.

The limp parachute

The next step in parachuting was the limp parachute. This had no form of stiffening to hold the parachute open as it hung beneath the balloon and had a trapeze bar instead of a basket. The first man to make a descent with one was an American tightrope-walker, Tom Baldwin, in 1887.

△ The US aeronaut Tom Baldwin making a descent with his limp parachute.

Midair rescue

Parachutes and balloons featured in open-air shows and exhibitions. In the early 1900s, an aerial showman called Captain Auguste Gaudron thrilled crowds in Britain with his daredevil band of parachutists – who did not use a harness. Particularly popular was the young Dolly Shepherd, who won fame with the first midair rescue. When her partner, making her first jump, could not free her parachute, Dolly took her down on hers.

△ Dolly Shepherd waits (left), trapeze in hand, to make an ascent. The parachute is stretched out in front of her. She hangs from the trapeze bar (right) as the balloon goes up.

Freefall

The "father" of skydiving was Leslie Irvin, an American parachutist. He made one of the first freefall parachute jumps, near Dayton, Ohio, in 1919 – against all technical and medical advice. His new, hand-operated chute revolutionized parachuting, saving countless lives in wartime and giving birth to a new sport.

△ A modern ram-air parachute.

Facts and records

△ The completion of a 24-man parachute stack in 1986, the result of a great deal of planning and organization as well as expert parachute control.

Record stack

The British Royal Marines performed parachute stacking in 1986 with 24 jumpers stacked one above the other. Jumping over Devon, in England, they took seven minutes to complete the stack.

Accuracy

The US Army Parachute Team, the Golden Knights, set a number of target jumping records at Yuma, Arizona, in 1978. Dwight Reynolds scored 105 dead-center strikes, and Bill Wenger and Phil Munden each scored 43 night time dead-centers.

In the world championships at Zagreb, Yugoslavia, in 1978, Jackie Smith (UK) achieved a record 10 consecutive dead-centers to win the gold medal.

Relative work

An American team formed a record 120-person formation in 1986 over Quincy, Illinois.

Base jumping

Parachute jumping off tall structures is called BASE jumping (Building, Antenna, Span, Earth). The practice has been banned in some countries because it does not allow enough time to deploy the parachute safely.

Glossary

Accuracy
Event in which competitors aim to land on a small target.

Aeroconical canopy
A round parachute, pointed at the top, used chiefly in training.

Altimeter
An instrument that tells the height above ground.

Canopy
The fabric part of a parachute.

Canopy relative work (CRW)
Linking up with parachutes open.

Dock
In relative work, to link up with another skydiver or with a group.

Freefall
Dropping free, before opening the parachute.

Frog position
A relaxed freefall position.

Ram-air canopy
A modern rectangular canopy. Air is rammed into cells at the front instead of being taken from underneath as with the traditional round parachutes.

Relative work
Combining with other skydivers in freefall.

Ripcord
Cable to open parachute.

Sport parachuting
The older name for skydiving.

Stable position
The basic student freefall position.

Stacking
CRW that involves stacking canopies one above the other.

Static-line jump
Method used by beginners to open parachute automatically after exit from aircraft.

Style
Individual competition for performing freefall maneuvers.

Terminal velocity
The maximum speed, about 120 mph (195 km/h), reached by any body falling through air.

Tracking
The ability to move in a horizontal direction as well as downward while freefalling.

Index